C000216197

Why not make a Beaded Amulet Purse?

Daphne J Ashby
& Jackie Woolsey

June 1998

Reprinted – November 1998
Reprinted – November 1999

DEDICATION

This booklet is written for and dedicated to all those
who have expressed enthusiasm for our beaded
purses and share our frustration at the lack of
printed instructions to pursue this addiction.

Other books by the same authors:

Ribbon Embroidery
> published by David & Charles
> Newton Abbott -   September 1996

*Creative Embroidery Techniques using Colour
through Gold*
> published by The Guild of
> Mastercraftsman Publications
> Lewes - June 1998

This booklet first published in the UK in June 1998
by Daphne J Ashby & Jackie Woolsey
Reprinted November 1998
Reprinted November 1999
The Firs, Dicks Mount, Burgh St. Peter, Beccles
NR34 0BU

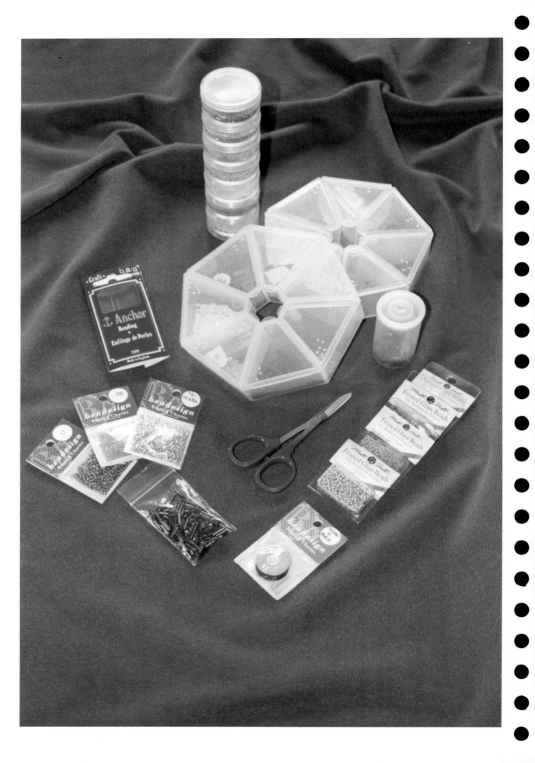

Why not make a Beaded Amulet Purse

Contents

INTRODUCTION

Over recent months, we have both become fascinated by (totally addicted to!) the craft of hand-threading beads to make miniature purses which hang around the neck.

Purchasing a kit to make the first purse, we were frustrated by the poor instructions which accompanied it; these were extremely difficult to follow, not to say impossible, but the end product, once Daphne had worked out a way of making the purse, proved a delight and set us on the road to pursuing the craft.

Despite combing shelves and catalogues, we could not find a simple book which covered the method we had worked out and so the idea evolved to publish our own explanatory leaflet and this then turned into a booklet when we realised how many gorgeous beads are available and the number of different designs which could be made up.

From the reaction of friends and strangers when they see the little purses being worn, this is likely to be a subject of interest to many people and, in order to help the beginner to start, we have divided this booklet into sections. We take the reader right through the making of a purse, from its collar, on which is hung the main body, on to the fringe at the base and then the necklace.

There follows a section which contains photographs and charts for purses which we have made to date, with suggestions for different fringes and necklaces. Finally we offer grid pages for you to work out your own designs.

This booklet is not, of course, exhaustive but we hope that it will enable you to make a start on this fascinating and decorative craft; beware, however, there is the danger that it may take you over.

A dictionary definition of an "amulet" is something worn as a charm against evil and so a beaded purse around the neck could be both decorative and useful!

Daphne J Ashby
and Jackie Woolsey

June 1998

GETTING STARTED

Beaded amulet purses are worked by making a collar of sets of seed and bugle beads, which are then formed into a circlet to which further rows of seed beads are added.

To make the body of the purse, rows of seed beads are threaded below the collar in a brick formation by following a charted pattern. The purse is closed at the lower edge and a fringe added, followed by a necklace at the top edge, with a decoration at the sides if desired.

The main thing you need to tackle this craft is time and patience but the end product is so decorative and satisfying that it is certainly worth the effort.

EQUIPMENT:

The primary requirement is, of course, beads and these are sold by several companies in the UK, each of whom puts a different number of beads into their packets. The purses which we illustrate and chart have been made mainly using beads from Beadesign and Mill Hill and the appropriate quantities have been stated in each design's requirement list.

As bead sizes vary, it is always a good idea to keep to one company for the beads used in the design you are working on and to buy sufficient at one time; either keep the wrapping or make a note of the reference number or name of the bead just in case this should be needed.

<u>Bugle beads</u>: These are elongated beads and come in a variety of lengths. The purses illustrated throughout this booklet have been made using bugle beads between 5 mm and 9 mm for collars, fringes and necklaces.

<u>Seed beads</u>: There are various suppliers of these particular beads, sometimes called embroidery beads, and there can be a frustrating variation in the sizes of these beads in some of the cheaper packets. When threading the beads, try to pick out those which are as similar in size as possible and avoid the obviously faulty or oversized. There is an enormous range of colours, lustres, pearls and bronzed beads and it is an enjoyable task making a choice for the chosen design.

Check carefully that the beads you are using are the same size; bugles from the same packet can vary in length and seed beads are not always uniform, which can cause the rows to become uneven.

<u>Beading needles</u>: These are available in packets of different sizes and the very finest have eyes which are very small and can be very difficult to thread, so a needle threader might also be a good investment.

<u>Beading thread</u>: This comes in a variety of thicknesses and it is suggested that the finest gauge and best quality is obtained. From experience, we would recommend using Beadesign Nymo 'D' which is available in black and white; logically, use black for dark beads, including gold, and white for the lighter/pastel shades and silver.

Small sharp pointed scissors.

Small tray (a shallow polystyrene dish from the supermarket can be useful for this) to hold the beads in current use; lining this with felt or fine velvet will make the whole process even easier and help to prevent the beads jumping about.

<u>Bead containers</u>: Look in craft shops or even fishing tackle shops for unusual containers which are suitable for holding beads. (See the example in the photograph facing page 1.) Film containers from photographic stores are also suitable.

Either a <u>6" ruler</u> or a <u>set of coloured pencils</u> will be helpful when following the designs from the charts. Move the ruler down one row at a time or simply colour each row in as you work.

JOINING A NEW THREAD:

Throughout the making of any purse, you will need to add new threads. Use long lengths of beading thread where possible, say 1.5 metres, and always finish each thread off whilst there is still sufficient left to weave back. Do this by weaving the old thread back through about 10 beads and start the new thread in the same way.

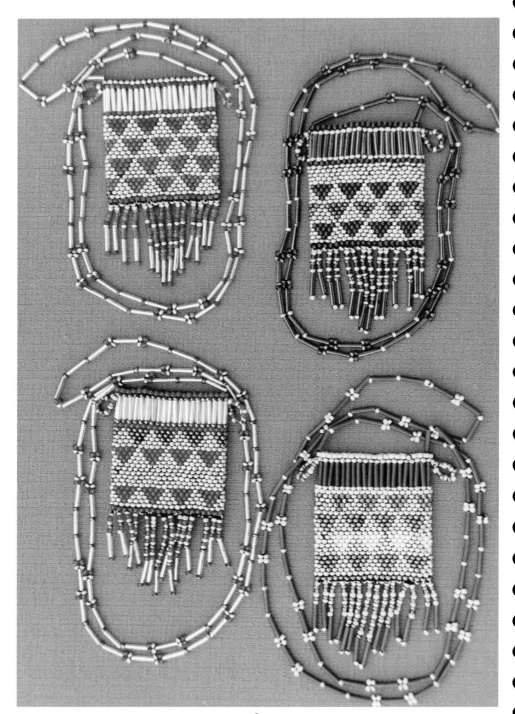

8

The next few pages of this booklet describe the making of a beaded amulet purse, which has been worked in four different combinations of colour shown in the photograph on the facing page.   The following are the requirements for the blue, cerise and turquoise version shown on the top left in the photograph and which is also featured on the cover of this booklet.

1 packet of gold bugle beads
2 packets of gold seed beads
1 packet each of three other colours of seed beads,
     in this case blue, cerise and turquoise
1 reel of black beading thread
Beading needles - 2 will be required for the necklace
Small sharp pointed scissors
Small tray to hold beads, preferably with felt lining

MAKING THE COLLAR

Select the colours for the top (collar) of the design: seed beads in gold, seed beads in blue and bugle beads in gold.

Cut a fairly generous length of beading thread (1.5 - 2 metres) and, using the beading needle, thread three beads on to the needle in the order:

1 blue seed bead
1 gold bugle bead
1 blue seed bead

and pull the needle through, leaving about six inches of thread hanging. Hold these beads firmly vertically between the finger and thumb of the left hand.

Pick up another set of three beads on the needle, pull the thread through the beads and fold the thread so that the two sets lay side by side between the fingers. Take the needle up through the first set again and down through the second set.

Each bead eventually has three threads passing through it, hence the need for a fine needle and fine thread.

* (1) Thread on another set of three beads.
  (2) Take the needle through the previous set
  (3) Then again through the set put on at (1) *

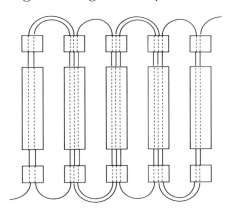

Tension the thread after adding each new set of beads, so that the row created does not flop about.   Repeat from * to * until you have 40 sets of beads altogether.

Bend the row round to form a circlet so that you can take the needle through the first set of beads and then back through set 40.   You now have a ring of beads which forms the basic collar and which you can hold over your index and middle fingers ready to start beading the main section.

Work a single row of gold seed beads on one edge of the collar using the following method:

Either using a new thread or with the needle and thread which is still attached to the collar:

** (1) Thread on a single seed bead
   (2) Take your needle up behind and over the thread
         between the next two beads of the previous row.
   (3) Go back down through the seed bead and pull the
         thread firmly. **

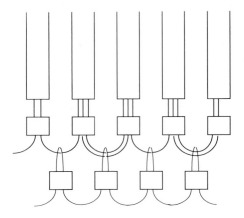

Repeat from ** to **until you have a complete round of gold seed beads.   Take your needle up through the first bead of the round and back down through the last bead of the round again.   It is <u>important</u> to finish each row and then start a new one; if you just carry on beading, it will upset your pattern.

Work a single row of gold seed beads in the same way around the top of the collar, so now you will have two rows of seed beads above and below the bugle beads, one in blue and one in gold.

THE MAIN BODY OF THE PURSE

Now, using the same method to attach the beads and starting at the top of the chart with Row 1, follow the chart given on page 14, finishing off each round before starting on the next.

When you have finished off your pattern, fasten off the thread ready to join up the lower edge of the purse.

CLOSING THE LOWER EDGE

Flatten the body of the purse, deciding which part of your design should be centralised on the front and which is the back. Working from one side, go through a bead of the last

Design for beaded purse on cover

Gold seed bead   )
Blue seed bead   )
)   Collar: 40 sets
Gold bugle bead   )
)
Blue seed bead   )
Gold seed bead   )

Key
   ▣   Gold
   ⊜   Turquoise
   ⬭   Cerise
   ○   Blue

Design requirements:
2 packets Gold seed beads
1 packet gold bugle beads
1 packet blue seed beads
1 packet turquoise seed beads
1 packet cerise seed beads

row on the front, thread a gold seed bead on to the needle, then go through the bead of the last row on the back. Repeat this from back to front and keep doing this, working in alternate directions along the lower edge. This will now be closed, giving you a row of gold seed beads from which to hang the fringe.

THE FRINGE

The actual fringe is made of seed beads and bugles, threading different numbers and making the strands different lengths. At this stage, larger beads could be added.

The fringes on the purses in the photograph facing page 9 were worked in accordance with the diagram shown on the next page - study the photographs for different bead colour combinations.

Join a thread so that it emerges at one end of the lower edge and pass the needle through the end joining bead. Thread all the beads required for the first strand of the fringe on to the needle and pull the thread through; then, missing the last bead, pass the needle and thread back through the rest of the beads again and through the bead on the purse from the opposite direction. Repeat for each strand.

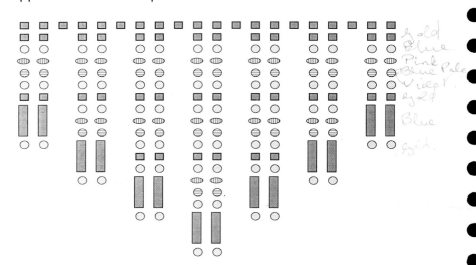

THE NECKLACE

When the fringe is complete, you are ready to make the necklace and, for this, you will need two beading needles with long threads.   Join the two at one top corner of the purse, weaving through the beads as before.

There are many ways of making the decorations at each corner where the thread is joined.   For this design, we used a circle of 16 seed beads as follows:

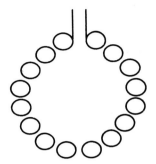

Now, using the two needles as described,   (*) on to one needle, thread:

1 gold bugle bead
1 blue seed bead
1 gold bugle bead
1 blue seed bead
1 gold bugle bead

Pass the second needle through the first five beads and then (**) thread one gold and one blue seed bead on to each needle.

With the second needle, go down through the two seed beads threaded on to the first needle and then back up through the two threaded on to the second needle.(**)

Thread both needles through a gold bugle bead and then repeat from (**) to (**) (*).

The whole process is then repeated from (*) to (*) as many times as necessary until the necklace is the required length.

Further suggestions for necklaces are shown in the photograph on page 37.

ENJOY WEARING YOUR FIRST BEADED PURSE

The remainder of this booklet contains photographs and charts of more designs for beaded amulet purses.

Designs for more Beaded Amulet Purses

Bead Design 2 - photograph top left on facing page

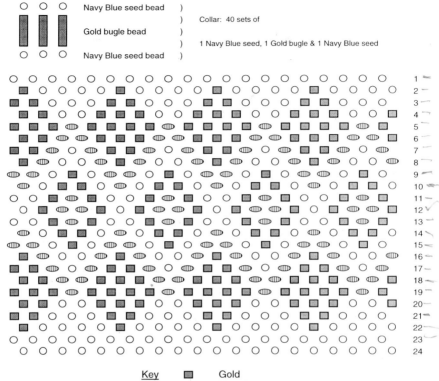

○ ○ ○	Navy Blue seed bead	)	
▌ ▌ ▌	Gold bugle bead	)	Collar: 40 sets of
○ ○ ○	Navy Blue seed bead	)	1 Navy Blue seed, 1 Gold bugle & 1 Navy Blue seed

Key
- ▣ Gold
- ○ Navy Blue
- ⬭ Red

Design requirements:
2 packets Gold seed beads
2 packets Navy Blue seed beads
1 packet Red seed beads
1 packet Gold bugle beads

Bead Design 3 - middle purse in photograph on page 20

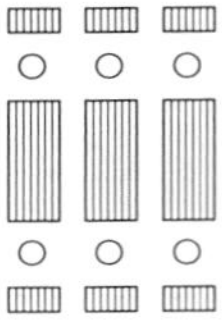

Green seed bead)
White seed bead)
)
Green bugle bead) Collar: 40 sets
)
White seed bead)
Green seed bead)

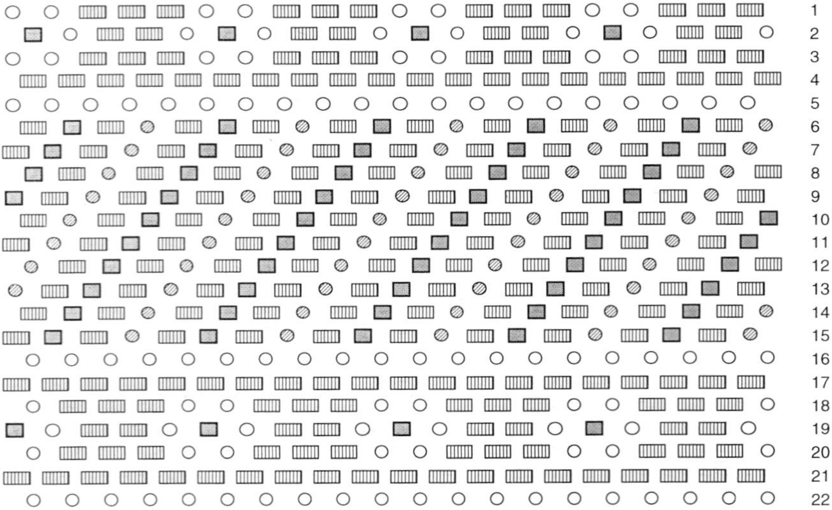
1
2
3
4
5
6
7
8
9
10
11
12
13
14
15
16
17
18
19
20
21
22

Key

- Gold
- White
- Green
- Blue

Design requirements:
1 packet gold seed beads
1 packet white seed beads
2 packets green seed beads
1 packet blue seed beads
1 packet green bugle beads

Bead Design 4 - right-hand purse in photograph on page 20

Green seed bead)
Green and gold seed beads alternately)
) Collar - 40 beads
Green bugle bead)
)

1
2
3
4
5
6
7
8
9
10
11
12
13
14
15
16
17
18
19
20
21
22
23
24
25

Key   ▨ Gold
       ⬭ Red
       ▥ Green

Design requirements:
1 packet gold seed beads
2 packets green seed beads
1 packet red seed beads
1 packet green bugle beads

Bead Design 5 - top left in photograph on facing page

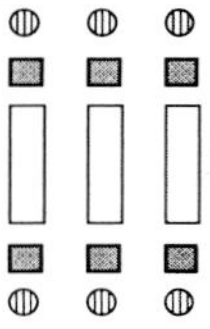

Dark blue seed bead)
Gold seed bead)
)
Dark blue bugle bead)   Collar: 36 sets
)
Gold seed bead)
Dark blue seed bead)

Between 5mm & 9mm

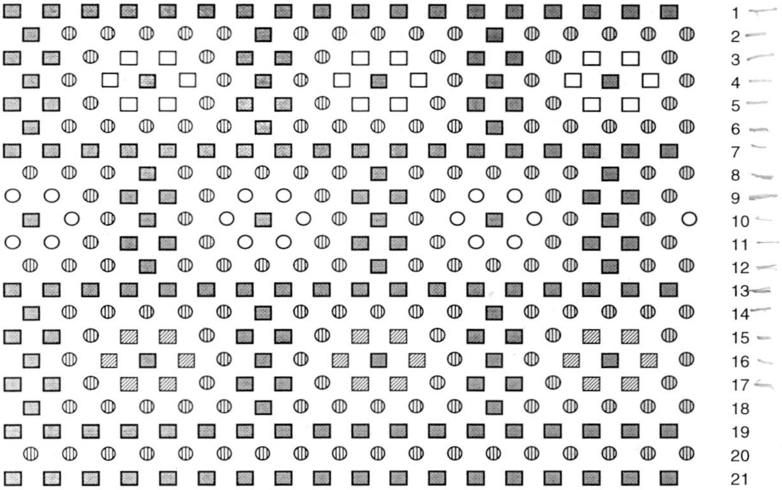

(rows numbered 1–21)

1
2
3
4
5
6
7
8
9
10
11
12
13
14
15
16
17
18
19
20
21

Key
 Gold
 Dark Blue
 Pink
 White
 Mauve

Design requirements
3 packets dark blue seed beads
2 packets gold seed beads
36 pink seed beads
36 white seed beads
36 mauve seed beads

Bead Design 6 - middle purse in photograph on page 24

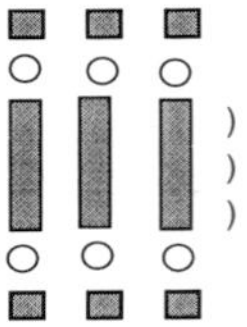

■ ■ ■	Gold seed bead	)		
○ ○ ○	Navy blue seed bead	)		
▌▌▌	Gold bugle bead	))))	Collar - 40 beads	
○ ○ ○	Navy blue seed bead	)		
■ ■ ■	Gold seed bead	)		

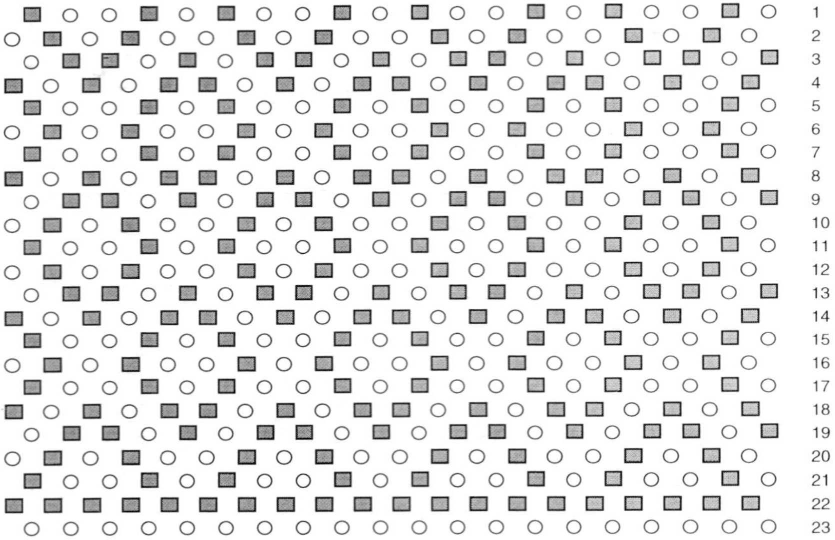

Rows numbered 1 to 23 (bead grid pattern).

Key   ■ Gold
       ○ Navy Blue

Design requirements:
1 packet gold bugle beads
2 packets gold seed beads
2 packets navy blue seed beads

Bead Design 7 - lower left purse in photograph on page 24

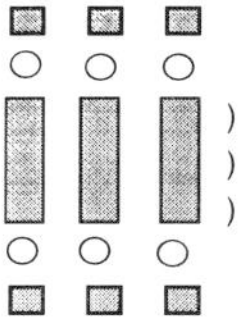

▨ ▨ ▨	Gold seed bead	)
○ ○ ○	Navy blue seed bead	)
▯ ▯ ▯)		)
▯ ▯ ▯)	Gold bugle bead	) Collar - 40 beads
▯ ▯ ▯)		)
○ ○ ○	Navy blue seed bead	)
▢ ▢ ▢	Gold seed bead	)

Bead chart rows numbered 1–24 (right side)

Key

▨	Gold
○	Navy Blue
▥	Green

Design requirements:
1 packet gold bugle beads
2 packets gold seed beads
1 packet navy blue seed beads
1 packet green seed beads

Bead Design 8 - top left purse in photograph on facing page

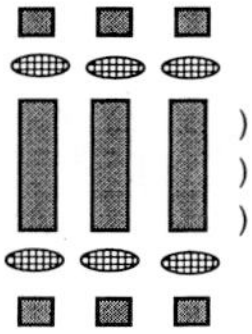

Gold seed bead)
Bronze seed bead)
Gold bugle bead) Collar - 42 beads
Bronze seed bead)
Gold seed bead)

1
2
3
4
5
6
7
8
9
10
11
12
13
14
15
16
17
18
19
20
21
22
23

Key
Gold
Bronze
Green-bronze

Design requirements:
1 packet gold bugle beads
2 packets gold seed beads
1 packet bronze seed beads
1 packet green-bronze seed beads

Bead Design 9 - lower purse in photograph on page 28

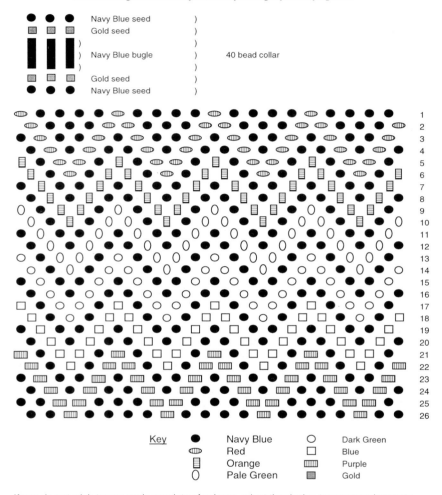

Key				
●	Navy Blue	○	Dark Green	
◖	Red	□	Blue	
▤	Orange	▥	Purple	
○	Pale Green	▨	Gold	

If you do not wish to use such a variety of colours, adapt the design to your requirements.

Design requirements:
1 packet navy blue bugle beads
2 packets navy blue seed beads
1/3 packet each of all other coloured seed beads

Bead Design 10 - top right purse in photograph on page 28

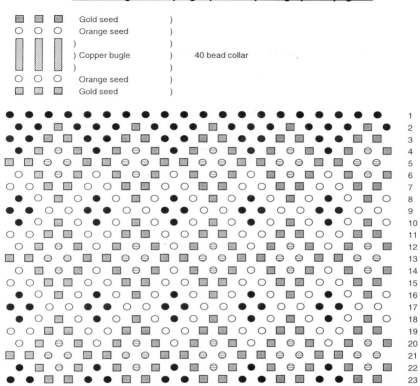

		Gold seed	)	
		Orange seed	)	
		)	)	
		) Copper bugle	)	40 bead collar
		)	)	
		Orange seed	)	
		Gold seed	)	

Key:

● Navy Blue
▨ Gold
⊖ Raspberry
○ Orange

Design requirements:
1 packet Copper bugle beads
2 packets gold seed beads
1 packet raspberry seed beads
1 packet orange seed beads
1 packet navy blue seed beads

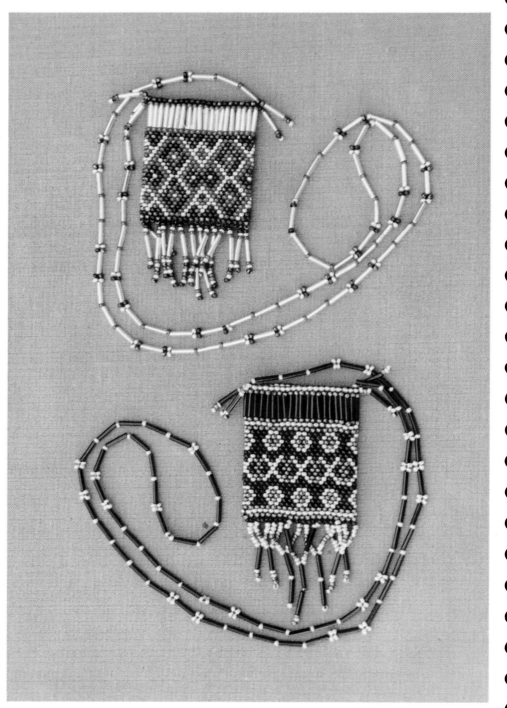

Bead Design 11 - top left purse in photograph on facing page
(with thanks to Carrie Evans)

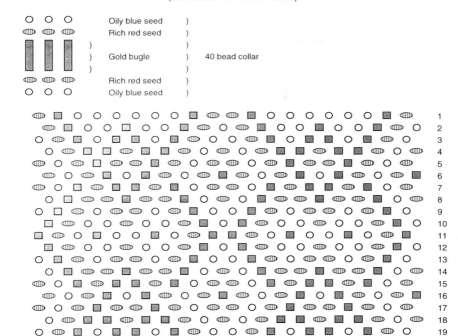

Oily blue seed)
Rich red seed)
)
Gold bugle)   40 bead collar
)
Rich red seed)
Oily blue seed)

Key ▨   Gold
     ⬭   Rich Red
     ○   Oily Blue

Design requirements:
1 packet gold bugles
2 packets blue seed beads
2 packets red seed beads
1 packet gold seed beads

Bead Design 12 - lower right purse in photograph on page 32
(with thanks to Pat Perry)

Gold seed)
Copper seed)
)
Black bugle) 40 bead collar
)
Copper seed)
Gold seed)

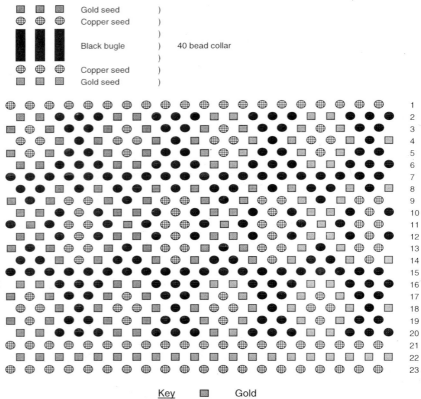

Key   Gold
      Copper
      Black

Design requirements
1 packet black bugles
2 packets gold seed beads
1 packet black seed beads
1 packet copper seed beads

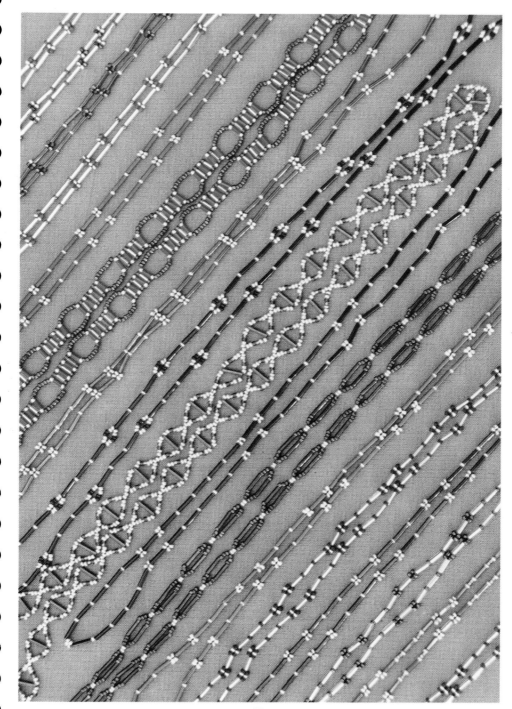

AND NOW:

If you are pleased with your first beaded amulet purse, why don't you experiment and see if you can design something a little more complicated?

We have included grid pages to enable you to design your own charts based on 36, 38, 40 and 42 bead collars.   Do photocopy and enlarge these pages to make the task easier.

Try: adding a flap
       changing the shape
       using more beads in the necklace
       creating new fringes

Three examples of the above ideas are shown in the purses photographed on the facing page to give you inspiration.   (A chart is given on the next page for the black, gold and bronze purse on the left.)

Good luck.

Daphne J Ashby and Jackie Woolsey

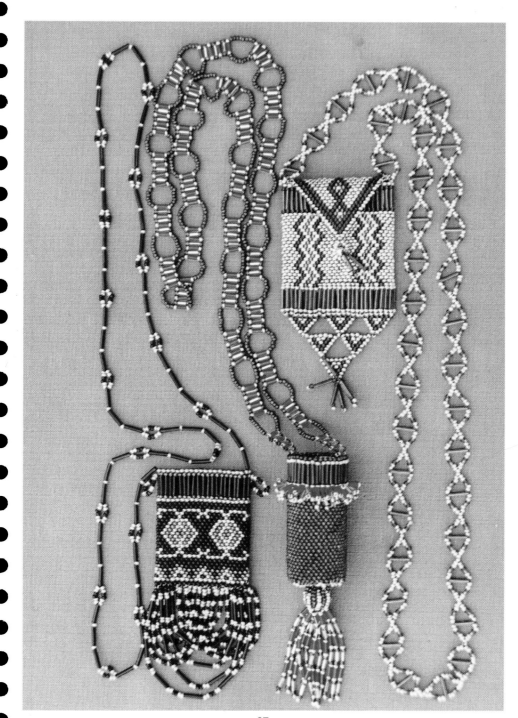

A more ambitious design! - lower left purse in photograph on page 37

Gold seed bead)
Bronze seed bead)
)
Black bugle bead) Collar - 40 beads
)
Bronze seed bead)
Gold seed bead)

Key
Gold
Black
Bronze

Design requirements:
1 packet black bugle beads
2 packets black seed beads
2 packets bronze seed beads
2 packets gold seed beads

Grid for 36 bead collar (use sideways)

Grid for 38 bead collar (use sideways)

Grid for 40 bead collar (use sideways)

Grid for 42 bead collar (use sideways)

Books about beads on the bookshelf:

"How to do Bead Work" by Mary White
Dover Publications Inc., New York

"Creative Bead Weaving" by Carol Wilcox Wells
Lark Books, Asheville, North Carolina

"The Beading Book" by Julia Jones
A & C Black, London

"The Bead Book" by Victoria Dutton
Random House UK Ltd., London

Bead supplies: The Beadesign and Mill Hill beads
mainly used in the illustrated purses are available at most
embroidery shops.   Two mail order suppliers are:

The Bead Merchant,
38 Eld Lane, COLCHESTER, Essex CO1 1LS

Creative Beadcraft Ltd (also trading as Ells & Farrer)
20 Beak Street, LONDON W1R 3HA